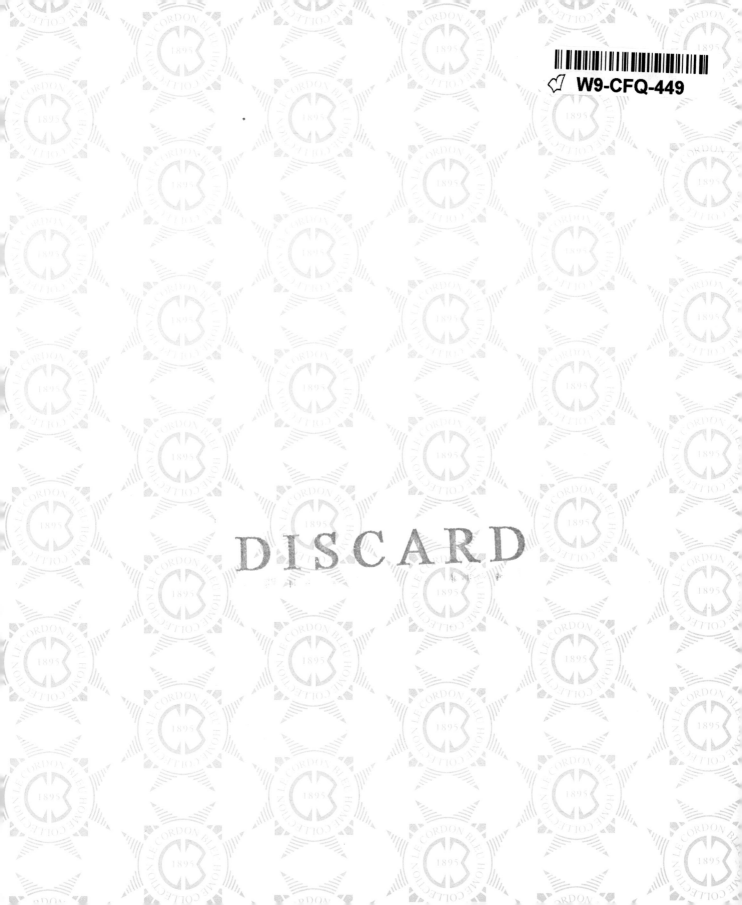

LE CORDON BLEU

HOME COLLECTION

SEAFOOD

PERIPLUS

contents

recipe ratings ✵ *easy* ✵✵ *a little more care needed* ✵✵✵ *more care needed*

Lobster bisque

Smooth, creamy bisques are thought to have their origins in Spain, where in the province of Biscay they may originally have been made with pigeons or quail until shellfish took over as the main ingredient in the seventeenth century.

*Preparation time **30 minutes***
*Total cooking time **30 minutes***
Serves 4

1 large or 2 small uncooked lobsters,
   1 1/2 lb. total
2 tablespoons olive oil
1/2 carrot, cut into cubes
1/2 onion, cut into cubes
1/2 small celery stalk, cut into cubes
2 1/2 tablespoons brandy
2/3 cup dry white wine
4 large tomatoes, peeled, seeded and quartered
1 bouquet garni (see Chef's tip)
6 cups fish stock
1/2 cup rice flour
2 egg yolks
1 tablespoon heavy cream
1 teaspoon finely chopped fresh tarragon

1 If you have bought live lobsters, kill them according to the method in the Chef's techniques on page 61. If you prefer not to do this, ask your fishmonger to do it for you.

2 Prepare the lobster following the method in the Chef's techniques on page 61. Heat the oil in a large saucepan, add the lobster pieces in their shell and stir for 2 minutes over high heat. Add the carrot, onion and celery, reduce the heat and cook for 2 minutes. Add the brandy and immediately ignite at arm's length, then allow the flames to subside or cover with a lid. Pour in the wine and stir to blend in any sticky juices from the saucepan bottom. Add the tomatoes, bouquet garni and stock and bring to a boil.

3 Using a slotted spoon, remove the lobster pieces from the stock, roughly break into small pieces using a knife and return to the saucepan with the rice flour. Stir to combine, bring to a boil and simmer for 10 minutes.

4 Pass the soup through a fine strainer, pressing the solids with the back of a spoon to extract all the juices, then discard the contents of the strainer, pour the liquid into a clean saucepan and season with salt and black pepper. The bisque should just coat the back of a spoon. If not, bring to a boil and simmer to reduce.

5 In a bowl, mix the egg yolks and cream together, stir in about 1/2 cup of the hot bisque, then pour back into the bisque. Check the seasoning and then reheat for 5 minutes, stirring continuously, without boiling. Sprinkle over the tarragon and serve in warm bowls or a soup tureen.

Chef's tip To make the bouquet garni, wrap the green part of a leek loosely around a bay leaf, a thyme sprig, some celery leaves and a few parsley stalks, then tie with string. Leave a long tail on the string for easy removal.

Ceviche

Ceviche originated in South America and is the perfect way to show off the freshest fish. The acidity of the lime dressing magically "cooks" the raw fish until it is opaque, just as if heat had been used.

Preparation time 55 minutes + 4 hours refrigeration
Total cooking time 1 minute
Serves 6

1 1/4 lb. snapper, sea bass or any firm white fish fillets,
** skin removed (see Chef's tips)**
juice of 6 limes
1 small onion, finely chopped
1 green bell pepper, halved, seeded and
** finely chopped**
1/2 red chili, seeded and finely chopped
1/2 cucumber, cut into 1/4-inch cubes
1 small avocado, peeled and cut into 1/4-inch cubes
4 tomatoes, peeled, seeded and diced
few sprigs fresh parsley or chervil, to garnish

WATERCRESS VINAIGRETTE
3 cups watercress leaves, tough stems removed
1 1/4 tablespoons white wine vinegar
1/3 cup olive oil

1 Cut the fish fillets into 1/4-inch-wide slices, pour over the lime juice, cover and refrigerate for about 2 hours.

2 Drain the fish, then add some salt and black pepper, the onion, bell pepper, chili, cucumber and avocado and mix gently to combine. Cover with plastic wrap and refrigerate for 1–2 hours. Chill 6 serving plates.

3 To make the watercress vinaigrette, add the watercress to a saucepan of boiling salted water and cook for about 1 minute, then drain and run under cold water. Pat dry with paper towels to remove excess water, then purée in a blender or food processor with the white wine vinegar and olive oil. Season with some salt and black pepper.

4 To serve, place a 3-inch egg ring or cookie or pastry cutter in the center of a chilled plate and spoon the ceviche into it until full, packing down lightly with the back of a spoon. Remove the ring and repeat on the other plates. Decorate the plates with the watercress vinaigrette and garnish with the diced tomato and parsley or chervil. Serve with some crusty bread.

Chef's tips If you can only buy a whole red porgy, snapper or sea bass, buy a 1 1/2-lb. fish and remove the bone yourself (see Chef's techniques, page 63).

For a creamier variation to this dish, add 1 cup coconut milk with the vegetables.

Gravlax

A Scandinavian method of curing salmon in salt, sugar and dill. The salmon is left to marinate for 1½ days and is then served with a traditional sweet dill and mustard dressing.

*Preparation time **1 hour + 36 hours refrigeration***
*Total cooking time **None***
Serves 10

❋ ❋

3³/4 lb. whole salmon fillet, skin on but scales removed
¹/3 cup rock, kosher or sea salt
¹/3 cup sugar
4 tablespoons chopped fresh dill
1¹/2 tablespoons black peppercorns, crushed
2 teaspoons coriander seeds, crushed
1 teaspoon ground allspice
6 tablespoons roughly chopped fresh dill leaves

DILL AND MUSTARD DRESSING
2 teaspoons sweet mustard (German) or 2 teaspoons
   grain mustard mixed with 2 teaspoons honey
2 teaspoons chopped fresh dill
2 teaspoons white wine vinegar or cider vinegar
1 cup vegetable oil

1 Wash the salmon fillet, dry it with paper towels and lay on a baking sheet or plate, skin side down. Mix together the salt, sugar, dill, peppercorns, coriander seeds and allspice and spoon over the fish. Cover with plastic wrap, top with a baking sheet and then a 1-lb. weight to press the salmon lightly (this could be cans spaced out along the fish). Refrigerate for 24 hours.

2 Remove the weight and covering, discard the solids from the marinade, then rinse the remaining marinade off with cold water and pat the salmon dry with some paper towels. Place on a clean baking sheet or plate, skin side down.

3 Press the dill leaves onto the salmon, then cover with plastic wrap and press well with your fingers to make the dill adhere. Refrigerate for 12 hours.

4 To make the dill and mustard dressing, mix all the ingredients except the oil together in a bowl with some salt and black pepper, then slowly drizzle the oil into the bowl, whisking to emulsify with the other ingredients.

5 Uncover the salmon, remove any excess dill, then lift onto a cutting board. With a long, thin-bladed knife held at an angle of 45 degrees and 2¹/2–3 inches from the tail, cut a slice toward the tail and continue working to produce short, thin slices. Serve with the dressing.

Chef's tip For a variation, try this beet and mustard mixture. Follow the recipe to the end of Step 2, then combine ¹/3 cup mustard seeds (soaked in cold water for 30 minutes, then drained) and 2 cups very finely chopped cooked beets. Press onto the salmon and continue as above.

Seafood paella

A classic Spanish dish consisting of rice and saffron, often combined with chicken, pork and chorizo, although here we use seafood only. The name is derived from the large, two-handled dish in which the paella is traditionally cooked and served.

Preparation time **45 minutes**
Total cooking time **45 minutes**
Serves 4

3 pinches of saffron threads
3 tablespoons olive oil
I large onion, sliced
I¹/₂ cups long-grain rice
3 tomatoes, peeled, seeded and roughly chopped, or
  14-oz. can diced tomatoes, drained
2 cloves garlic, crushed
2¹/₄ cups chicken or vegetable stock
³/₄ lb. mussels, scrubbed and beards removed
  (see page 62)
16 large shrimp, shells on
I cooked crab in its shell, cleaned and cut
  into quarters, or 4 cooked crab claws
  in their shells (see Chef's tips)
¹/₂–³/₄ lb. small clams or cockles, well washed
¹/₄ lb. firm white fish fillets, skin removed and
  cut into I¹/₄-inch pieces
²/₃ cup frozen baby peas
I red bell pepper, cut into I-inch lengths
  and thinly sliced

1 Place the saffron threads in a small bowl and soak in 2 tablespoons hot water.

2 Heat the oil in a paella pan or heavy-bottomed frying pan, 12–14 inches in diameter, add the onion and cook for 3–4 minutes, or until soft. Add the rice and saffron and cook, stirring, for 2 minutes. Add the tomatoes, garlic and stock and bring to a boil. Reduce the heat and stir in half the mussels, shrimp, crab, clams and fish with all the peas and red bell pepper. Season well with salt and black pepper.

3 Arrange the remaining seafood on top and cover with a piece of waxed paper and a lid. Cook over low heat for 30 minutes, or until the rice is tender and the liquid has been absorbed. Don't stir the paella while it cooks, as this will break up the fish and make the finished dish look messy. If the liquid has been absorbed but the rice is not cooked, add a little extra water and continue cooking until the rice is cooked through. Discard any unopened mussels and serve immediately.

Chef's tips Paella is traditionally served directly from the pan. If you are using a frying pan, check that it is deep enough (1¹/₄–2 inches) to hold the liquid.

To clean a crab, remove the stomach sac and gray spongy fingers (gills).

Coquilles Saint-Jacques mornay

Coquilles Saint-Jacques, the French term for scallops, literally means "Saint James's shells." Here the scallops are baked in the half shell beneath a crown of piped potato and a Gruyère cheese sauce.

Preparation time **25 minutes**
Total cooking time **45 minutes**
Serves 4

❋ ❋

8 sea scallops, preferably in their shells
¹/2 cup finely grated Gruyère cheese

DUCHESSE POTATOES
2 lb. baking potatoes, peeled and cut into pieces
1¹/2 tablespoons unsalted butter
2 egg yolks
pinch of freshly grated nutmeg

MORNAY SAUCE
1 tablespoon unsalted butter
2 tablespoons all-purpose flour
1 cup milk
1 egg yolk
¹/2 cup grated Gruyère cheese

1 To prepare the scallops, follow the method in the Chef's techniques on page 62. Place the scallops flat on a cutting board and slice each one into 3 circles, leaving the orange roe (if available) whole. Cover and refrigerate until needed.

2 If you have purchased the scallops in their shells, scrub the shells, place in a saucepan of cold water and bring to a boil. Simmer for 5 minutes, then drain and leave the shells to cool and dry. If you do not have scallops in their shells, you may use either scallop shells purchased in a specialty cookware shop or 4 small shallow gratin dishes.

3 To make the duchesse potatoes, put the potatoes in a large saucepan of salted, cold water. Cover and bring to a boil, reduce the heat and simmer for 15–20 minutes, or until the potatoes are tender to the point of a sharp knife. Drain, return to the saucepan and shake over low heat for 1–2 minutes to remove excess moisture. Mash or push through a fine strainer into a bowl, then stir in the butter and egg yolks and season with nutmeg, salt and black pepper. Spoon the mixture into a pastry bag with a ⁵/8-inch star tip. Preheat the oven to 400°F.

4 To make the mornay sauce, melt the butter in a heavy-bottomed saucepan over medium-low heat. Sprinkle over the flour and cook for 1 minute without allowing it to color, stirring continuously with a wooden spoon. Remove from the heat and slowly add the milk, blending thoroughly. Return to the heat and bring slowly to a boil, stirring constantly. Lower the heat and cook for 3–4 minutes, or until the sauce coats the back of a spoon. Remove from the stove and stir in the egg yolk and cheese, then season with salt and black pepper.

5 Pipe shell shapes or small overlapping circles of duchesse potato to form a border around the edge of each shell or dish. Place on a baking sheet that has a rim so that the round edge of each shell rests on the rim to prevent the filling from running out. Place a sliced scallop and whole roe, if available, in each rounded shell, season with salt and black pepper and spoon over the mornay sauce. Sprinkle the cheese over the sauce and bake for 12–15 minutes, or until golden brown.

Smoked trout pâté

*A stylish but easy-to-make pâté, with a combination of fresh and smoked trout. For a variation,
you could use smoked and fresh salmon or mackerel.*

*Preparation time **30 minutes + cooling +***
1 hour refrigeration
*Total cooking time **5 minutes***
Serves 6

1 tablespoon white wine vinegar
1 bay leaf
4 white peppercorns
1/4 lb. fresh trout fillet, skin on
3/4 lb. smoked trout fillet, skin off
3/4 cup cream cheese
1/3 cup unsalted butter, softened
1 tablespoon fresh lemon juice
4 fresh parsley, chervil or dill sprigs,
   to garnish

1 Put the wine vinegar, bay leaf, white peppercorns and
1/2 cup water in a shallow saucepan and bring slowly to
a simmer. Put the fresh trout, skin side down, in this
poaching liquid, cover and gently cook the trout for
3–4 minutes, or until cooked through. Allow to cool in
the liquid. Using a fish turner or spatula, lift the trout
carefully onto a plate and remove and discard the skin
and any bones.

2 Put the fresh and smoked trout in a food processor
and process to a smooth purée. Add the cream cheese,
butter, lemon juice and some salt and black pepper and
process until all the ingredients are thoroughly
combined. Divide the pâté among six 1-cup ramekins,
about 3 inches in diameter, and place in the refrigerator
for 1 hour. To serve, garnish with a parsley, chervil or dill
sprig and accompany with melba toast.

Chef's tip This makes an excellent cocktail dip if served
soft at cool room temperature. Alternatively, pipe it
onto small rounds of toast as a canapé and garnish with
a dill or chervil sprig.

Sardines with walnut and parsley topping

A crisp walnut topping gives these broiled fresh sardines a lovely texture. They can be served as a main course or appetizer with warm olive oil, lemon wedges, arugula leaves and plenty of fresh bread.

Preparation time 40 minutes
Total cooking time 20 minutes
Serves 4

WALNUT AND PARSLEY TOPPING
2/3 cup unsalted butter
4 shallots, finely chopped
2 cloves garlic, crushed
4 tablespoons fresh white bread crumbs
1 cup walnuts, finely chopped
2 teaspoons finely chopped fresh parsley

**16 fresh sardines, 1³/4 oz. each, cleaned
   and scales removed**
2 tablespoons all-purpose flour
¹/4 cup olive oil
2 tablespoons olive oil, warmed, to serve
lemon wedges, to serve
few arugula leaves, to serve

1 To make the walnut and parsley topping, melt the butter in a saucepan over moderate heat. Add the shallots and garlic, cover and cook for about 3 minutes, or until soft and translucent. Remove from the stove, season with some salt and black pepper, then add the bread crumbs, walnuts and parsley and mix thoroughly.
2 Preheat the broiler to high. Wash the sardines, then dry well on paper towels. Put the flour on a plate or piece of waxed paper and season well with salt and black pepper. Pour the oil on a separate plate. One at a time, roll the sardines in flour to coat them, then shake off the excess flour. Dip into the oil, coating on both sides, then transfer half the sardines to a baking sheet or shallow roasting pan. Place under the broiler and cook for 3 minutes on each side. Remove the first batch to a plate and keep warm while you cook the second batch.
3 Sprinkle the walnut and parsley topping over the sardines and press firmly onto the skin. Return to the broiler, in two batches, and cook until the topping is golden brown.
4 Place the sardines on a large serving plate or individual plates and drizzle the warm olive oil around the sardines on the bare areas of the plate. Complete with some black pepper, the lemon wedges and a few arugula leaves.

Coulibiac

A Russian fish pie packed with salmon, rice, hard-boiled eggs and mushrooms, then wrapped in puff pastry to form a pillow shape. A great dish for a party, especially when served with warm beurre blanc (white butter sauce).

Preparation time **50 minutes + 15 minutes refrigeration**
Total cooking time **1 hour 40 minutes**
Serves 8

¹/4 *cup long-grain rice*
4 eggs
3 tablespoons unsalted butter
6 small scallions, finely sliced
3 large shallots, finely chopped
4¹/2 cups finely chopped mushrooms
juice of ¹/2 lemon
1 lb. salmon fillet, skin on
1 lb. prepared puff pastry
2¹/2 tablespoons finely chopped fresh dill
1 egg yolk
¹/3 cup plain yogurt

COURT BOUILLON
1 small carrot, roughly chopped
1 small onion, roughly chopped
1 bay leaf
4 fresh parsley stalks
1 fresh thyme sprig
6 black peppercorns
large pinch of salt
2 tablespoons white wine vinegar

1 Cook the rice until tender, then drain well. Hard-boil 3 of the eggs for 10 minutes, put in a bowl of iced water to cool quickly, then coarsely grate or finely chop.

2 Melt half the butter in a saucepan and add the scallions. Cover and cook for 4 minutes over low heat until soft and translucent. Season and set aside.

3 Melt the remaining butter, add the shallots and cook gently for 2 minutes. Add the mushrooms, lemon juice, salt and pepper and cook until the mushrooms are dry.

4 To make the court bouillon, put all the ingredients except the vinegar in a saucepan with 6 cups water. Bring to a boil, then simmer, covered, for 15 minutes. Add the vinegar and simmer for 5 minutes.

5 Add the salmon to the court bouillon and poach, covered, for 5 minutes. Remove from the heat, uncover and let the salmon cool in the liquid before transferring to a plate. Remove the flesh in large flakes from the skin and cover with plastic wrap. Discard any skin and bones.

6 Cut the pastry in half and, on a lightly floured surface, roll out one-half to a ¹/8-inch-thick rectangle. Transfer to a baking sheet without a lip and trim down to a rectangle big enough to contain the salmon, about 9 x 14 inches. Wrap and chill the trimmings, layering them flat. Leaving a 1 inch border on all sides, spread the rice in the center of the pastry. Sprinkle over ¹/2 tablespoon of dill, then the salmon, salt and pepper, mushroom mixture, egg and scallions in separate layers.

7 Beat the remaining egg and brush over the pastry border. Roll remaining pastry to about 18 x 12 inches, then pick the pastry up on the rolling pin and place over the filling. Press the edges together to seal the top and bottom, then trim neatly and brush with egg. Roll out the reserved trimmings and cut strips to decorate the pie. Lay them on as a lattice and place the pie in the refrigerator for 10–15 minutes.

8 Preheat the oven to 400°F. Beat the egg yolk and any remaining egg together and brush over the pie. Wipe off any egg from the baking sheet and make 3 small holes down the center of the pie with a skewer. Bake for 30 minutes, until risen, crisp and golden.

9 Stir the remaining dill into the yogurt and serve with slices of the coulibiac.

Bouillabaisse

Fishermen in Marseilles made this fragrant soup using fish that were difficult to sell. These were tossed into a simmering pot, hence the name bouillabaisse, from "bouillir" (to boil) and "abaisser" (to reduce). You can use any combination of the fish below in the soup, and increase the amount of one fish if another is not available.

Preparation time 1 hour
Total cooking time 1 hour 10 minutes
Serves 4–6

☼ ☼

1 John Dory or turbot, about 1 lb., bones removed
   and reserved (see pages 62–63)
2 sole, about 1 lb. total, bones removed and reserved
1 lb. monkfish, bones removed and reserved
1 halibut, about 1 lb., bones removed and reserved
1 lb. conger eel, cut into pieces, or 12 littleneck clams,
   well-washed, or sea scallops
1/3 cup olive oil
2 cloves garlic, finely chopped
pinch of saffron threads
1 each carrot, fennel bulb and leek (white part only),
   cut into julienne strips
24 thin slices baguette, for croûtes
3 cloves garlic, cut in half, for croûtes
chopped fresh basil, to garnish

SOUP

1 small leek, onion and fennel bulb, thinly sliced
1 celery stalk, thinly sliced
2 cloves garlic
2 tablespoons tomato paste
2 cups white wine
pinch of saffron threads
2 fresh thyme sprigs
1 bay leaf
4 fresh parsley sprigs

ROUILLE SAUCE

1 egg yolk
1 tablespoon tomato paste
3 cloves garlic, crushed into a paste

pinch of saffron threads
1 cup olive oil
1 baked potato, about 1/2 lb.

1 Season the fish and eel, clams or scallops with salt and black pepper and toss with half the oil, the garlic, saffron, carrot, fennel and leek. Cover and refrigerate.

2 To make the soup, heat the remaining oil in a stockpot over high heat, add the reserved bones and cook for 3 minutes. Stir in leek, onion, fennel, celery and garlic and cook for 2 minutes, then mix in the tomato paste and cook for 2 minutes. Pour in the white wine and simmer for 5 minutes. Finally, add 4 cups water, saffron and herbs and simmer for 20 minutes. Pass through a strainer, pressing down to extract as much juice as possible, and discard the solids. Put the soup in a saucepan and simmer for 15 minutes until slightly thickened, skimming to remove any foam that floats to the surface.

3 To make the rouille, whisk the egg yolk in a small bowl with the tomato paste, garlic, saffron and some salt and black pepper. Continue to whisk while slowly pouring the oil into the mixture. Press the flesh of the potato through a strainer and whisk into the sauce.

4 Lightly toast the baguette slices under a preheated broiler, cool, then rub both sides with the cut sides of the half cloves of garlic to make garlic croûtes.

5 Cut each fish fillet into six pieces and add to a large pot with the eel, clams or scallops and julienned vegetables. Pour the hot soup over and simmer for 7 minutes, or until the fish is cooked. Remove the fish and vegetables and place in an earthenware or metal dish. Whisk 3 tablespoons of the rouille into the soup to thicken it a bit, then pour the soup over the fish and sprinkle with the basil. Serve with the garlic croûtes and the remaining rouille.

Garlic shrimp

Ideal as an appetizer or light summer lunch, serve this Spanish-inspired dish with lots of crusty bread to soak up the lemony garlic butter.

*Preparation time **20 minutes***
*Total cooking time **10 minutes***
Serves 4
❋

1/4 lb. curly endive, escarole or frisée
1 red chili, seeded and very thinly sliced
1 tablespoon fresh chervil leaves
24 large shrimp, shells on
2 teaspoons vegetable or olive oil
4 cloves garlic, crushed
1/2 cup unsalted butter, cut into cubes
finely grated zest and juice of 1 lemon
1 tablespoon finely chopped fresh parsley

1 Mix together the endive, escarole or frisée, chili and chervil leaves and pile onto the center of 4 plates.

2 Shell and devein the shrimp, removing the heads but leaving the tails intact, following the method in the Chef's techniques on page 60. Place the shrimp on a plate and season lightly with salt and black pepper. Heat the oil in a large, heavy-bottomed frying pan over medium-high heat. Add the shrimp and fry for about 1 minute on each side, or until cooked through. Remove and keep warm.

3 Add the garlic to the pan and cook for 1 minute, then add the cubes of butter and cook for 4 minutes, or until the butter is nut brown. Remove from the stove and add the lemon zest and juice and the parsley.

4 Quickly shake the pan once or twice to combine all the ingredients, then add the shrimp and toss briefly to warm through. Immediately arrange the shrimp around the salad on the plates. Pour any remaining pan juices over the top.

Whole baked salmon with watercress mayonnaise

Baked in foil to retain the salmon's flavor and moist texture, this impressive centerpiece is the perfect dish for a large summer gathering, served with new potatoes and summer vegetables.

*Preparation time **1 hour 10 minutes**
    + 1 hour refrigeration*
*Total cooking time **40 minutes***
Serves 10–12

**1 whole salmon, 3–3 1/2 lb., cleaned and scales removed
    (ask your fishmonger to clean the fish
    and remove the scales)
1 small onion, thinly sliced
1 small bay leaf
1 fresh thyme sprig
5 fresh parsley sprigs
1/3 cup dry white wine
watercress sprigs, to garnish
lemon wedges, to garnish**

WATERCRESS MAYONNAISE
**4 cups watercress, tough stems removed
1 1/4 cups whole-egg mayonnaise
few drops of lemon juice**

1 Lift up the gill flap behind the cheek of the salmon head and, using kitchen scissors, remove the dark, frilly gills. Repeat on the other side of the fish. If any scales remain, hold the tail and, using the back of a knife, scrape the skin at a slight angle, working toward the head. Trim the fins. Cut across the tail to shorten it by half, then cut a V shape into the tail. Wash the salmon under cold water and open it on the belly side where the fishmonger has slit it. Remove the blood vessel lying along the backbone using a spoon. Rinse and wipe inside and out with paper towels.

2 Preheat the oven to 350°F. Butter a piece of foil large enough to wrap around the fish and place on a large baking sheet. Lay the salmon just off center and place the onion and herbs inside the belly. Season with salt and black pepper, then pour over the wine. Quickly cover with foil and seal the edges tightly.

3 Bake for 30–40 minutes, or until the fish feels springy and firm to the touch. Open the foil and leave to cool. Remove the flavorings and lift the salmon onto waxed paper, draining off any liquid. Prepare the salmon for serving following the Chef's techniques on page 63, then cover with plastic wrap and refrigerate for 1 hour, or until needed.

4 To make the watercress mayonnaise, add the watercress to a saucepan of boiling salted water and cook for 1 minute, then drain and run under cold water. Pat dry with paper towels to remove excess water, then purée in a blender or food processor. Beat the purée gradually into the mayonnaise. If it is too dry, add a few drops of lemon juice. Season with salt and black pepper.

5 To serve, decorate the fish with some mayonnaise and serve the remainder separately. Garnish with the watercress sprigs and lemon wedges.

Crab cakes

These crispy crab cakes make a perfect light lunch with salad, or you can make lots of small ones to serve as appetizers at a barbecue or as part of a summer picnic.

*Preparation time **55 minutes + 20 minutes cooling + 30 minutes refrigeration***
*Total cooking time **20 minutes***
*Serves **4–6***

2 tablespoons vegetable oil
I onion, finely chopped
2 cloves garlic, crushed
I¹/₂ tablespoons grated fresh ginger
I small red bell pepper, halved, seeded and
   cut into fine dice
8 scallions, finely chopped
I lb. crabmeat, drained well if frozen
   or canned
2 teaspoons Tabasco sauce
2 tablespoons chopped fresh flat-leaf parsley
3 tablespoons fresh bread crumbs
¹/₂ teaspoon Dijon mustard
I egg, beaten
I²/₃ cups seasoned flour, sifted, for coating
I¹/₄ cups fresh bread crumbs, for coating
²/₃ cup grated Parmesan, for coating
2 eggs, for coating
oil, for deep-frying
lemon wedges, to serve

1 Heat the oil in a frying pan and add the onion, garlic and ginger. Cook for 1 minute, then add the bell pepper and scallions and cook for 2 minutes, or until soft. Transfer to a plate and leave for 20 minutes to cool completely. When cool, stir in the crabmeat, Tabasco, parsley, bread crumbs, mustard and some salt and black pepper. Add the egg and bind together.

2 Divide mixture into 4, 6 or 12 portions, depending on desired size of cakes. Using lightly floured hands and a lightly floured surface, shape into cakes. Put on a baking sheet, cover and refrigerate for 30 minutes, or until firm.

3 Place the flour on a large piece of waxed paper. Combine the bread crumbs and Parmesan on another piece of paper. Beat the eggs in a shallow dish. One at a time, place cakes in the flour, then pat off any excess. Put in the eggs and use a brush to help coat. Remove with a fish turner or spatula, lay on the bread crumbs and Parmesan and toss in these. Reshape the cakes, pressing the crumbs on, then place on a baking sheet.

4 Heat oil to a depth of ¹/₂ inch in a nonstick frying pan and cook the cakes, in batches, over medium heat for 1–2 minutes each side, or until golden. Drain on crumpled paper towels and serve with lemon wedges.

Chef's tip To keep the crab cakes warm and crisp, place on a wire rack in a warm oven.

Seafood risotto

In this recipe, baby clams, shrimp, mussels, crab and fish fillets provide a host of different textures and flavors set in a creamy saffron risotto. Any combination of fresh seafood could be used instead.

Preparation time **35 minutes**
Total cooking time **1 hour**
Serves 4

1/4 lb. baby clams
1 lb. red mullet or sea bass fillet
1/4 lb. shrimp, shells on
3/4 cup dry white wine
5 tablespoons olive oil
1 small onion, finely chopped
1/2 lb. mussels, scrubbed and beards removed
  (see page 62)
1 bay leaf
1 fresh thyme sprig
2 cups fish stock
pinch of saffron threads
1 clove garlic, finely chopped
1 1/4 cups arborio rice
2/3 cup grated Parmesan
grated zest of 1 lime
1 1/2 tablespoons crème fraîche or sour cream
3 1/2 oz. crabmeat, drained well if frozen or canned
few fresh basil leaves, to garnish

1   Scrub and rinse the clams under cold running water to get rid of grit, then discard any that are open or damaged. Remove any pin bones from the fish following the Chef's techniques on page 63. Shell and devein the shrimp, reserving the heads and shells, following the method in the Chef's techniques on page 60.

2   Put the clams in a saucepan, add half the white wine and cook, covered, for 3 minutes, or until the clams open. Drain through a strainer lined with cheesecloth or damp paper towels and reserve the liquid. Discard any clams that have not opened, then remove the clams from their shells and cover with plastic wrap. Discard the shells.

3   In a saucepan, heat 1 tablespoon of the oil, add half the onion and cook over low heat for 4 minutes, or until soft and transparent. Add the remaining wine, mussels, bay leaf and thyme and cook, covered, for 2–3 minutes, or until the mussels open. Drain as for the clams, reserving the liquid. Discard any unopened mussels, then remove from their shells and cover.

4   In a saucepan, place the stock, 2 cups water, clam and mussel liquid, shrimp heads and shells and saffron. Bring to a boil, simmer for 10 minutes, then pass through a fine strainer. Return to the rinsed pan; keep warm.

5   In a saucepan, heat 1 tablespoon of the oil, add the garlic and remaining onion and cook over low heat for 2–3 minutes, or until soft. Add the rice and stir for 2 minutes with a wooden spoon, making sure it is completely coated with the oil, then pour in enough stock to just cover the rice. Cook over low heat, stirring continuously, until the stock is absorbed. Continue to cook for 15–20 minutes, pouring in a little stock and allowing it to be absorbed before adding more. The risotto is ready when the rice is just tender but still *al dente* (there should also be a little stock left over). Remove from the heat, fold in the Parmesan, lime zest and crème fraîche and cover. Reserve the remaining stock.

6   Meanwhile, preheat the broiler and brush the fish with olive oil. Season with salt and pepper and broil, skin side up, for 2 minutes, or until cooked. Cover and keep warm. Heat the remaining oil in a saucepan and toss the shrimp over high heat for 2 minutes, or until pink and cooked through.

7   Pour the remaining stock into a saucepan, add the mussels, clams and crab and just heat through. Mix the seafood and its liquid into the risotto and transfer to a serving dish. Place the fish and basil on top.

Smoked trout gougère

Here, a cheese-flavored crown of choux pastry holds a filling of smoked trout, leek, tomato and dill. For a variation, you could try a mixture of fish such as salmon and monkfish, or perhaps some shellfish.

Preparation time **35 minutes**
Total cooking time **45 minutes**
Serves 6

CHOUX PASTRY
1 1/4 cups all-purpose flour
1/3 cup unsalted butter, cut into cubes
pinch of salt
4 eggs, lightly beaten
1 cup coarsely grated Cheddar
1 teaspoon Dijon mustard

FILLING
1/2 lb. smoked trout fillet
1 tablespoon unsalted butter
1 small leek or 4 scallions, white part only, sliced
2 tablespoons all-purpose flour
3/4 cup milk
1 large tomato, peeled, seeded and cut into
　1/2-inch strips
1 teaspoon chopped fresh dill

1 egg, beaten
1 tablespoon grated Parmesan
1 tablespoon lightly toasted fresh bread crumbs
1 tablespoon unsalted butter, melted
chopped fresh dill, to garnish

1 Brush six 5 3/4 x 1 1/4-inch round gratin dishes with melted butter and refrigerate to set.
2 To make the choux pastry, sift the flour onto a clean sheet of waxed paper. Put 1 cup water, the butter and salt in a saucepan. Heat until the butter and water come to a boil. Remove from the heat and add the flour all at once, then mix well using a wooden spoon. Return to the heat and stir until a smooth ball forms and the dough leaves the sides of the saucepan, then remove from the heat and place the dough in a bowl. Using a wooden spoon or electric mixer, add the eggs to the dough a little at a time, beating well after each addition. The mixture is ready to use when it is smooth, thick and glossy. Beat in the cheese and mustard and season well with salt and black pepper. Cover and set aside.
3 To make the filling, place the smoked trout flat in a shallow saucepan and pour in enough cold water to cover. Slowly bring to a boil, covered, then turn off the heat and leave for 7 minutes.
4 Melt the butter in a deep saucepan, add the leek and cook over low heat for 3 minutes to soften. Sprinkle over the flour, stir in using a wooden spoon and cook for 1 minute. Remove from the heat, mix in the milk, then return to the heat and bring to a boil, stirring constantly. Simmer for 1 minute, or until the mixture thickens.
5 Preheat the oven to 400°F. Lift the fish from its cooking liquid, pat dry with paper towels, then use a fork to take the fish lightly off its skin in flakes. Gently stir the flakes into the filling with the tomato, dill and some salt and black pepper.
6 Fill a pastry bag with a 1/2–5/8-inch tip with the pastry. Pipe a circle around the outside of the base of the prepared dishes, then a second circle on top to cover the side of the dish. Spoon the filling into the middle of the choux circles and brush the top of the pastry lightly with the beaten egg. Combine the Parmesan and bread crumbs, sprinkle over the filling, then drizzle with the melted butter. Place on a baking sheet and bake for 15–20 minutes, or until the pastry is risen and crisp. Sprinkle with dill to garnish.

Chef's tips You can also spoon in the pastry to cover the sides of the dish and give a more peaked surface.

　To make one large gougère, use a deep 8-inch round ovenproof dish and bake for 30–35 minutes.

Fish and chips

Tradition at its best: firm white fish that flakes at the touch of a fork, cooked in a crisp batter and served with homemade chips—French fries. For best results, make sure the fish is very fresh and eat piping hot.

Preparation time **20 minutes + 30 minutes standing**
Total cooking time **20 minutes**
Serves 4

1 1/4 lb. baking potatoes, peeled
oil, for deep-frying
1/4–1/2-lb. pieces firm white fish fillet, skin removed
2–3 tablespoons seasoned flour
lemon wedges, to garnish

BATTER
1 1/4 cups cornstarch
1 1/4 cups all-purpose flour
1 tablespoon baking powder
1 1/4–2 cups beer

1   Cut the potatoes into batons 1/4–1/2 inch wide, 1/2 inch deep and 2 1/2–3 inches long. Put in a bowl and cover with cold water.

2   To make the batter, sift the cornstarch, all-purpose flour, baking powder and some salt and black pepper into a bowl and make a well in the center. Gradually pour in the beer, using a wooden spoon to beat it into the flour, until the mixture becomes a smooth batter the consistency of cream (the amount of liquid you need will depend on the flour you use). Cover and leave for 30 minutes at room temperature.

3   Meanwhile, fill a deep fryer or heavy-bottomed saucepan one-third full of oil and heat to 315–325°F (a cube of bread dropped into the oil will brown in 30 seconds). Drain the fries and pat dry, then fry until the bubbles subside and the fries form a thin, light golden skin. Lift out the fries, allowing excess oil to drip back into the fryer, and transfer to crumpled paper towels.

4   Increase the temperature of the oil to 350°F (a cube of bread dropped into the oil will brown in 15 seconds). Wash the fish and dry thoroughly on paper towels. Place the seasoned flour on a plate and coat the fish, shaking off the excess. Dip the fish into the batter until it is evenly coated, then lift out using fingers or forks to allow any excess mixture to drip off. Lower the fish into the fryer or saucepan and fry, in batches if necessary, for 5 minutes, or until golden and crisp. Do not crowd the saucepan or the temperature will be lowered. Remove and drain on crumpled paper towels. Season with salt, place on a wire rack and keep warm.

5   Put the fries in the oil again and fry until golden and crisp. Remove and drain, season with salt and serve with the fish, lemon wedges and tartar sauce or ketchup.

Sole Véronique with potato galettes

*A classic French recipe using white grapes in a white wine sauce to accompany poached lemon sole.
Here the dish is served on crisp potato galettes.*

Preparation time **1 hour**
Total cooking time **1 hour 15 minutes**
Serves **4**

POTATO GALETTES
**1 lb. baking potatoes, peeled and cut into
    uniform pieces**
4 egg whites
clarified butter, for frying

8 sole fillets, 1/4 lb. each, skin removed
2 shallots, finely chopped
1/3 cup dry white wine
3/4 cup fish stock
1 cup seedless white grapes
1 1/4 cups heavy cream

1 To make the potato galettes, put the potatoes in a large saucepan of salted, cold water. Cover and bring to a boil, then reduce the heat and simmer for about 15–20 minutes, or until the potatoes are tender to the point of a sharp knife. Drain, return to the saucepan and shake over low heat for 1–2 minutes to remove excess moisture. Mash or push through a fine strainer, season with salt and black pepper and allow to cool.

2 Meanwhile, wash the sole and dry well on paper towels. Fold the skinned side under at each end of the fillets to give 8 fillets about 4 inches long. Butter a shallow 12 x 8 1/2-inch ovenproof dish and sprinkle half the shallots over the bottom. Place the sole fillets on the shallots, drizzle with 1 tablespoon each of the wine and the stock and season lightly with some salt and black pepper. Cover with plastic wrap and set aside in the refrigerator.

3 Put the grapes in a saucepan of boiling water and cook for 15 seconds, then drain and plunge into iced water to cool. Remove from the water, peel away their skins and reserve the grapes and skins separately.

4 Preheat the oven to 350°F. In a bowl, whisk the egg whites until they hold stiff peaks. Stir one-quarter of the egg whites into the potato then, using a spatula or large metal spoon, gently fold in the remaining egg white.

5 Place clarified butter to a depth of 1/2 inch in a large, heavy-bottomed frying pan and place over moderate heat. Lightly oil the inside of a 3-inch round plain egg ring or cookie or pastry cutter and place in the pan. Put a 1/4-inch layer of the potato inside the ring. Gently loosen around the sides with a thin-bladed knife and lift the ring away. Repeat to fill the pan, leaving enough space between the galettes to turn them over. Fry for 5 minutes on each side, or until golden brown. Drain on crumpled paper towels, then remove to a wire rack in a low oven and keep warm.

6 Put the remaining shallots, the wine and the stock in a saucepan. Add the grape skins, bring to a boil, then simmer for 20 minutes, or until the mixture is syrupy. Meanwhile, bake the sole for 10–12 minutes, or until the flesh is opaque and cooked through. Stir the cream into the sauce and simmer for 5 minutes, or until syrupy, then strain into a clean saucepan, discarding the grape skins. Strain the cooking liquid from the fish into the sauce, reduce again until it is syrupy, then add the grapes and warm through.

7 To serve, place a galette on each plate, arrange 2 sole fillets on top and coat with the sauce.

Chef's tip For a richer finish, mix together 3 tablespoons lightly whipped cream and 1 egg yolk. Coat the sauced fillets with the mixture, then broil until golden brown.

Smoked salmon and leek terrine with sauce verte

Beautifully light but with a good depth of flavor, this dish makes a perfect appetizer or lunch. Cooking the leeks in fish stock helps them to press together better, and makes it easier to slice the terrine.

*Preparation time **1 hour + 4 hours refrigeration***
*Total cooking time **20 minutes***
Serves 10

6 cups fish stock
30 very small whole leeks, tough green leaves and
  roots removed
10–15 large spinach leaves, stems removed
1– 1 1/4 lb. long slices smoked salmon
arugula leaves, to garnish

SAUCE VERTE
3 1/2 cups watercress, tough stems removed
3/4 cup fresh chervil leaves, chopped
3/4 cup fresh dill leaves, chopped
3/4 cup fresh parsley leaves, chopped
few drops of lemon juice
1 1/3 cups crème fraîche or sour cream

1 In a large saucepan, bring the fish stock to a boil. Put the leeks in the stock, reduce the heat and simmer gently for 20 minutes, or until tender. Drain well, then set aside to cool.

2 Blanch the spinach in boiling water for 30 seconds. Drain, then plunge into iced water. Carefully lift the leaves out individually and place on paper towels or a cloth towel and pat dry.

3 Line a 4-cup, 8 1/2 x 4-inch terrine mold with plastic wrap, then line the base and sides with some of the smoked salmon, allowing a long overhang at one end. Add a layer of spinach, allowing for an overlap over one side of the terrine.

4 Tightly pack 2 layers of leeks lengthwise into the bottom of the lined terrine and season well, then add a layer of half the remaining salmon, followed by one layer of leeks and seasoning. Cover with the remaining salmon and top this with 2 layers of leeks and seasoning. Fold over the salmon and spinach overhangs to enclose the filling and cover with plastic wrap. Cut a piece of cardboard to fit inside the terrine, cover it twice with foil and place a 2-lb. weight on top (this can be cans). Refrigerate for 4 hours.

5 To prepare the sauce verte, put the watercress, herbs and a little water into a blender and blend to a fine purée. Push through a coarse strainer, add the lemon juice and salt and black pepper and fold in the crème fraîche or sour cream. Cover with plastic wrap and place in the refrigerator until ready to serve.

6 To serve, slice the terrine and arrange on plates with a spoonful of the sauce verte and some arugula leaves to garnish.

Fish minestrone with pesto

A twist on the classic Italian soup, with the addition of scallops, shrimp and a dash of cream. The pesto is stirred through at the end, and any extra can be tossed through pasta for a great midweek dinner.

*Preparation time **1 hour 15 minutes***
*Total cooking time **15 minutes***
Serves 4

4 sea scallops
12 large shrimp, shells on
4 cups fish stock
2 1/2 tablespoons olive oil
1 small onion, finely diced
1 small carrot, diced
1/2 rutabaga, peeled and diced
1 small turnip, peeled and diced
1 potato, peeled and diced
1/4 celery root, peeled and diced
1/2 cup small pasta shapes, such as soup pasta
1/4 cup cut-up green beans (1/4-inch lengths)
1 zucchini, diced
3 tablespoons heavy cream
1/2 cup drained, cooked or canned flageolet beans
few fresh chervil sprigs, to garnish

PESTO
4 cloves garlic
1/3 cup pine nuts, toasted
1/3 cup grated Parmesan
1/2 cup fresh basil leaves
3/4 cup fresh parsley leaves
3/4 cup olive oil

1 To prepare the scallops, follow the method in the Chef's techniques on page 62. Place the scallops flat on a cutting board and slice each one into 3 circles, leaving the orange roe (if available) whole. Shell and devein the shrimp, following the method in the Chef's techniques on page 60. Then, cover and refrigerate the scallops and shrimp until needed.

2 To make the pesto, put all the ingredients in a blender or food processor and blend to a smooth thick mixture. Transfer the pesto to a clean jar with a screw lid and cover the surface with a layer of oil to stop it from oxidizing.

3 Place the stock in a small pan and bring to a boil. Heat the oil in a large pan and add the onion, carrot and rutabaga. Cover and cook over low heat for 2 minutes, or until soft and translucent. Add the turnip and potato, pour in the boiling stock, season lightly with salt and bring to a boil. Add the celery root and pasta and simmer for 5 minutes, or until the vegetables are just tender. Add the beans and the zucchini and cook for 2 minutes.

4 Remove from the heat and stir in the cream and flageolet beans. Add 3 tablespoons of the pesto, the scallops and shrimp and mix gently to blend in the pesto. Season with salt and black pepper, then return to the stove just to bring back to a boil (do not continue to cook or the scallops and shrimp will overcook and toughen). Garnish with chervil sprigs to serve.

Chef's tip Leftover pesto will keep in the refrigerator for up to 1 week or it can be stored in the freezer in an airtight container. Toss with pasta, use as a salad dressing or place on cooked mussels in the half shell and quickly broil until bubbling.

Creamy and salsa oysters

Two versions of classic oyster dishes. The creamy version is made with cream, white wine and bacon and is flashed under the broiler to give a golden topping. If you prefer less heat, just omit the chili. The salsa oysters are not cooked and come with a fiery tomato, red onion and lime dressing.

Preparation time **50 minutes**
Total cooking time **15 minutes (Creamy version)**
Serves 4

24 oysters

CREAMY
2 teaspoons Tabasco sauce
1/4 lb. bacon slices
4 egg yolks
1/3 cup white wine
1/3 cup heavy cream, lightly whipped
1/2 red chili, seeded and finely chopped
1 tablespoon olive oil
1 small red bell pepper, cut into matchsticks

OR

SALSA
2 cups peeled, seeded, and diced tomatoes
1 red onion, finely chopped
juice of 2 limes
1 teaspoon Tabasco sauce
1 teaspoon roughly chopped fresh cilantro
1 tablespoon roughly chopped fresh flat-leaf parsley
fresh cilantro leaves, to garnish

salad leaves or crushed ice, to serve

1 Shuck the oysters following the method in the Chef's techniques on page 60. Add the oysters to their liquid in the bowl and refrigerate until needed. Clean the deeper half of the shells thoroughly and discard the flat halves.

2 To make the creamy oysters, add half the Tabasco to the oysters before refrigerating. Place the bacon in a small pan, cover with cold water, bring to a boil and simmer for 4 minutes. Drain, then run under cold water to remove excess salt. Place the bacon on paper towels to drain, then cut into matchsticks.

3 Put the egg yolks, wine and remaining Tabasco in a heatproof bowl over a saucepan of simmering water, ensuring the bowl is not touching the water. Whisk vigorously until the mixture has increased to three or four times the original volume and leaves a trail across the surface when lifted on the whisk. Remove the bowl from the pan, whisk until it cools to room temperature, then fold in the cream and chili and set aside.

4 Preheat the broiler. Heat the oil in a saucepan and fry the bacon until golden, then add the bell pepper and cook for 1 minute, or until soft but not colored. Heat the oysters and their juices in another saucepan over low heat for 1 minute. Do not overheat or the oysters will toughen. Put the warm oysters back in their shells and place in a flameproof dish (a layer of rock salt underneath will help them stay balanced). Pour over the juices and place the bacon and bell pepper mixture on top. Spoon the egg mixture over and place under the broiler for 2 minutes, or until golden. Serve immediately.

5 To make the salsa, mix together all the ingredients except the whole cilantro leaves with some salt and black pepper. Cover with plastic wrap and set aside for 20 minutes at room temperature. Place an oyster in each shell and spoon over some juices and a little salsa, then garnish with a cilantro leaf. Arrange on a bed of salad leaves or crushed ice.

Creamy oysters (top) and salsa oysters

Spaghetti marinara

Meaning "mariner's style," the name of this pasta dish originated from fishermen's wives throwing their husbands' daily catch into a quick tomato, garlic, herb and olive oil sauce.

*Preparation time **35 minutes***
*Total cooking time **50 minutes***
Serves 4

3 tablespoons olive oil
1 onion, finely chopped
2 cloves garlic, crushed
1 tablespoon tomato paste
2 (14-oz.) cans diced tomatoes
2 fresh thyme sprigs
1 bay leaf
1/2 lb. tuna fillet, skin removed and cut into 3/4-inch cubes
1/2 lb. cleaned squid tubes, sliced into 1/4-inch-wide rings
1/2 lb. crabmeat, drained well if frozen or canned
4 tablespoons chopped fresh basil
1 lb. spaghetti

1 In a large saucepan, heat 2 tablespoons of the olive oil, add the onion and garlic and cook for 4 minutes, or until the onion is soft and translucent. Stir in the tomato paste and cook for another minute. Add the tomatoes, thyme and bay leaf, season with salt and black pepper, then bring to a boil, lower the heat and simmer for about 25 minutes.

2 Heat the remaining oil in a large frying pan, add the tuna and toss over high heat for about 3 minutes, or until lightly cooked. Lift out the tuna using a slotted spoon and drain in a colander over a bowl. Reheat the oil remaining in the pan, add the squid rings and toss over high heat for 3 minutes, or until opaque, then remove and add to the tuna to drain.

3 Remove and discard the thyme and bay leaf from the tomato sauce, then add the tuna cubes, squid rings, crabmeat and 3 tablespoons of the basil. Stir gently to combine without breaking up the fish and season with some salt and black pepper. Remove from the heat and keep warm.

4 Meanwhile, bring a large saucepan of salted water to a boil. Add a splash of oil to prevent the pasta from sticking and cook the spaghetti according to the manufacturer's instructions. Drain well.

5 Serve the spaghetti on warm plates and spoon the marinara sauce on top. Sprinkle with the remaining basil and serve immediately.

Chef's tip Frying the seafood at a high temperature will seal it, give a good flavor and allow it to hold its shape.

"Lasagna" of salmon with tomato and spinach

There is no pasta in this special dish, but the effect is like a lasagna, with layers of pink salmon, dark green spinach leaves, and white and tomato sauces, making for a stunning dinner-party recipe.

Preparation time *1 hour*
Total cooking time *1 hour 15 minutes*
Serves 4

4 thick center cuts salmon fillet, 1/4–1/2 lb. each, skin removed and cut into 3 slices horizontally (ask your fishmonger to do this)
1/3 cup olive oil
2 onions, finely chopped
2 lb. ripe tomatoes, peeled, seeded and diced
2 cloves garlic, crushed
bouquet garni (see Chef's tip)
3 tablespoons unsalted butter
1 1/2 lb. spinach, tough stems removed
small pinch of grated nutmeg
12 small black olives, halved and pitted, to garnish
few fresh chervil sprigs, to garnish

BEURRE BLANC (WHITE BUTTER SAUCE)
3 shallots, finely chopped
1 1/4 cups dry white wine
3 tablespoons cider vinegar
1 tablespoon heavy cream or crème fraîche
3/4 cup unsalted butter, cut into small cubes and chilled
2 tablespoons finely chopped fresh chives

WHITE SAUCE
1 tablespoon unsalted butter
2 tablespoons all-purpose flour
1 cup milk

1 Separate the slices of salmon, brush with olive oil, cover and place in the refrigerator. Heat the oil in a saucepan, add the onion, cover and cook for 4 minutes, or until soft and translucent. Stir in the tomatoes, garlic, bouquet garni and some salt and pepper. Cook for about 40 minutes, stirring occasionally, until the mixture is thick. Discard the bouquet garni, reseason and keep warm.

2 To make the beurre blanc (white butter sauce), put shallots, wine and vinegar in a saucepan, bring to a boil and cook to reduce by one-quarter. Add cream and remove from the heat, then whisk in the butter a piece at a time to form a creamy, flowing sauce that coats the back of a spoon. Strain into a bowl, stir in chives, cover with plastic wrap and place over a saucepan of warm water.

3 To make the white sauce, melt the butter in a heavy-bottomed saucepan over low-medium heat. Sprinkle the flour over the butter and cook for 1–2 minutes without allowing it to color, stirring continuously with a wooden spoon. Remove the saucepan from the heat and slowly add the milk, whisking to avoid lumps. Return to medium heat and bring to a boil, stirring constantly. Cook for 3–4 minutes, or until the sauce coats the back of a spoon. Cover and keep warm. Preheat the broiler.

4 Melt the butter in a large frying pan or wok, add the spinach and toss over high heat for 2 minutes, or until wilted. Add nutmeg, salt and black pepper and place in a strainer over a bowl to allow moisture to drain. Season the fish and broil for 1 minute each side.

5 To serve, take 4 plates and place a salmon slice on each one. Using half the spinach, spread a layer on each slice, then add half the white sauce, followed by half the tomato sauce. Cover with another slice of fish, the remaining spinach, white and tomato sauces, and finish with the remaining salmon. Spoon the beurre blanc around the base of the plate and garnish with the olive halves and chervil leaves.

Chef's tip To make a bouquet garni, wrap the green part of a leek loosely around a bay leaf, a thyme sprig, some celery leaves and a few parsley stems, then tie with string, leaving a long tail for easy removal.

Snapper with fennel en papillote

Cooked in a parcel of waxed paper or foil to retain all the juices and flavors, the white wine, basil leaves and gentle anise aroma of fennel infuse the sweet snapper.

*Preparation time **40 minutes***
*Total cooking time **35 minutes***
Serves 4

2 snapper fillets, 3/4 lb. each (see page 63)
2 large fennel bulbs
4 tablespoons unsalted butter
16 fresh basil leaves
4 tablespoons dry white wine
4 teaspoons Pastis or Ricard (optional)

1 Wash the fish, dry on paper towels and refrigerate until needed. With a small, sharp knife, trim off the small stalks at the top of the fennel bulbs, keeping the leaves and discarding the thick stalks. With a large, sharp knife, cut the bulb in half from the top down through the root, then cut away and discard the root. Cut the fennel into 1/4-inch-thick slices.

2 Heat the butter in a saucepan, add the fennel slices, cover and cook over low heat for 25 minutes, or until tender to the point of a sharp knife. Remove from the stove and season with some salt and black pepper. Preheat the oven to 425°F.

3 Fold a piece of waxed paper or foil in two, then cut out a large half teardrop shape 2 inches bigger than the fish. Open the paper or foil out and you should have a heart shape. Repeat to make 4 total, then lay the shapes flat and brush with melted butter. Spoon the fennel onto one side of each heart and spread to the size of the fish. Place a fish fillet on top and lightly season with salt and black pepper. Arrange 4 basil leaves on each piece of fish, then sprinkle each one with a tablespoon of white wine and a teaspoon of Pastis or Ricard. Top with the reserved fennel leaf sprigs.

4 Immediately fold the empty side of paper or foil over and seal the edges by twisting and folding tightly. Place on a baking sheet or in a shallow ovenproof dish and bake for 5–8 minutes. Place the packets on serving plates and let your guests open them to release the aroma.

Chef's tip Other fish can be cooked by this method, such as perch, mackerel or cod. The cooking times will vary according to the thickness and shape of the fish.

Thai green fish curry

This fish curry is prepared with an easy-to-make homemade green curry paste, which gives a fresh, authentic Thai taste. Serve with fragrant steamed jasmine rice.

*Preparation time **15 minutes***
*Total cooking time **20 minutes***

Serves 4–6

GREEN CURRY PASTE
1 cup coconut milk
8 small green chilies (bird's-eye), halved and seeded
1 lemongrass stalk, chopped
2 tablespoons lime juice
1 tablespoon fresh galangal or ginger slices
1 teaspoon ground coriander
1/2 teaspoon ground cumin
5 shallots or scallions, chopped
3 kaffir lime leaves, chopped

1 tablespoon sunflower oil
1/2 mild red or green chili, seeded and
  cut into shreds
1 tablespoon drained green peppercorns in brine,
  plus 1 teaspoon brine
1 teaspoon sugar
1 2/3 cups coconut milk
5 kaffir lime leaves
1 1/2 lb. firm white fish fillets, skin removed and cut
  into 1 1/2-inch cubes

1 tablespoon fish sauce
2 tablespoons roughly torn basil leaves, for garnish

1 To make the green curry paste, blend all the ingredients in a blender or food processor, scraping down the sides of the bowl occasionally, until the mixture is smooth and forms a thick paste. If it is too thick, add a little more coconut milk or a few drops of sunflower oil. Put in a bowl, cover and set aside.

2 In a wok or large frying pan, heat the sunflower oil, then add the chili and toss for about 4 minutes, or until lightly golden. Add the peppercorns, brine, sugar and coconut milk, bring to a boil and simmer for about 3 minutes.

3 Add 4 tablespoons of the green curry paste, the lime leaves and the fish. Simmer for 5–10 minutes, or until the fish is cooked. Remove and discard the lime leaves, season with salt, black pepper and the fish sauce and keep warm.

4 To serve, lift out the fish into a warm serving dish and spoon the sauce over. Sprinkle with the torn basil leaves and serve.

Chef's tip The leftover curry paste can be stored in an airtight container in the freezer and used to make a fish, chicken or vegetable green curry.

Seafood pie

*A classic family dish, this seafood pie is made with white fish, mussels and shrimps in a light wine
sauce and topped with a purée of potato that is baked until lightly golden in the oven.*

Preparation time **50 minutes**
Total cooking time **1 hour 10 minutes**
Serves 6

1 lb. mussels, scrubbed and beards removed
   (see page 62)
1/4 lb. shrimp, shells on
4 tablespoons unsalted butter
2 shallots, finely chopped
1 leek, white part only, cut into julienne strips
1 cup dry white wine
2 cups milk
1 onion, studded with 1 whole clove
bouquet garni (see Chef's tips)
11/4 lb. mixed firm white fish fillets such as sole,
   cod and halibut, skin removed and cut into
   11/4-inch cubes
1/4 cup all-purpose flour
2 lb. baking potatoes, peeled and cut into
   uniform-sized pieces
additional 31/2 tablespoons unsalted butter
1 egg yolk
4 tablespoons heavy cream
small pinch of grated nutmeg

1 Place the mussels in a cool place covered with a
damp cloth. Shell and devein the shrimp, following the
method in the Chef's techniques on page 60.
2 In a saucepan, melt 2 tablespoons of the butter over low
heat, add the shallots, cover and cook for 2–3 minutes, or
until soft. Add the leek and cook, uncovered, for 2 minutes,
then add 1 tablespoon of wine and simmer until the
liquid evaporates. Place in a shallow, oval 11 x 8-inch
ovenproof dish.
3 Put the mussels and remaining wine in a saucepan,
cover, bring slowly to a boil and cook for 2–3 minutes, or

until all the mussels are open. Discard any unopened
mussels. Drain, reserving the cooking liquid, then
remove the mussels from their shells and scatter into
the dish. Pass the liquid through a strainer lined with
cheesecloth or damp paper towels and set aside.
4 Add the milk, onion and bouquet garni to a saucepan,
bring to a bare simmer and cook for 5 minutes. Remove
the onion and bouquet garni and add the cubes of fish,
shrimp and reserved mussel liquid. Heat to just
simmering and poach the seafood for 2 minutes. Drain,
reserving the liquid and keeping it hot, and add the
seafood to the dish.
5 Melt the remaining 2 tablespoons butter in a
saucepan over low heat, sprinkle in the flour and cook,
stirring, for 1 minute without coloring. Remove from
the heat and blend in the hot poaching liquid. Return to
medium heat, bring to a boil, stirring constantly, and
cook for 3–4 minutes, or until it thickens and coats the
back of a spoon. Season, then pour over the fish. Cover
and refrigerate.
6 Preheat the oven to 350°F. Put the potatoes in a
saucepan of salted, cold water, cover and bring to a boil,
then reduce the heat and simmer for 15–20 minutes, or
until the potatoes are tender to a sharp knife. Drain,
return to the saucepan and shake over low heat for
1–2 minutes to remove excess moisture. Mash or push
through a fine strainer back into the pan, then beat in
the 31/2 tablespoons butter, egg yolk and cream. Season
with nutmeg, salt and black pepper, spoon into a pastry
bag with a large star tip and pipe a pattern over the fish.
Or spread the potato, then use a fork to peak. Bake for
30 minutes, or until light golden.

Chef's tips To make a bouquet garni, wrap the green
part of a leek loosely around a bay leaf, a thyme sprig,
some celery leaves and a few parsley stems, then tie with
string, leaving a long tail for easy removal.

Seafood gumbo

A thick, spicy soup from the American South with its origins in Creole cuisine, influenced by African and French cooking. The original meaning of gumbo was "okra," and this vegetable is what thickens the dish.

Preparation time **45 minutes**
Total cooking time **35 minutes**
Serves 4

12 large shrimp, shells on
¼ cup long-grain rice
2½ tablespoons vegetable oil
2 large onions, chopped
1 celery stalk, finely chopped
2 cloves garlic, crushed
1 red bell pepper, diced
1 green bell pepper, diced
3 tablespoons tomato paste
4 cups fish stock
2 teaspoons chopped fresh oregano
1 cooked crab in its shell, cleaned and cut
**   into quarters, or 4 cooked crab claws**
**   in their shells (see Chef's tip)**
2 cups sliced okra (½-inch-thick slices)
¼ lb. snapper fillet, skin removed and cut into
**   1½-inch pieces**
1 teaspoon Tabasco sauce
1 teaspoon Worcestershire sauce
2 scallions, finely chopped, to garnish

1 Shell and devein the shrimp, leaving the tails intact, following the method in the Chef's techniques on page 60. Cook the rice in boiling salted water for 10 minutes, or until tender, then drain and leave to cool.
2 In a large frying pan, heat the oil. Add the onions, celery, garlic and bell peppers. Stir over medium heat for 5 minutes, or until soft but not colored. Mix in the tomato paste and stir for 1 minute, then add the stock, oregano and crab and simmer for 5 minutes. Gently stir in the okra, season lightly, cover and simmer for 15–20 minutes, or until the okra is tender.
3 Remove the pan from the stove and lift out the crab pieces, crack them with the base of a small heavy pan, and remove the meat as whole pieces if possible. Discard the shells, cover the crabmeat and keep warm.
4 Skim the gumbo to remove any oil or foam, then return to the stove, add the fish and shrimp and simmer for 2 minutes. Add Tabasco and Worcestershire sauces, stir in the rice and bring the gumbo back to a simmer. Taste and add more salt, pepper or sauces if necessary (you want a good hint of chili). To serve, ladle into bowls and garnish with scallions. Serve with bread.

Chef's tip To clean a crab, remove the stomach sac and gray spongy fingers (gills).

Lobster à l'Américaine

In this famous lobster dish, the lobster is cooked in the shell in a tomato and wine sauce. There is much dispute on the origin of the name—whether it should be Armoricaine, the ancient name for Brittany, or Américaine, after a French chef who had worked in the United States.

*Preparation time **30 minutes***
*Total cooking time **50 minutes***
Serves 4

4 lobsters, 1 lb. each, or 2 lobsters, 1 3/4–2 lb. each
1/3 cup vegetable oil
3 tablespoons unsalted butter
1 onion, diced
1 carrot, diced
2 celery stalks, diced
1/2 cup dry white wine
2 1/2 tablespoons brandy
2 cups fish stock
3 tablespoons tomato paste
1 lb. ripe tomatoes, halved and seeded
1 bouquet garni (see Chef's tips)
fresh parsley sprigs, to garnish

1 If you have bought live lobsters, kill them according to the method in the Chef's techniques on page 61. If you prefer not to do this, ask your fishmonger to do it.

2 Prepare the lobster following the method in the Chef's techniques on page 61. To fry the lobster claws and tails, heat the oil in a large frying pan and add the claws and tails. Fry quickly, turning with long-handled tongs, until they change color from blue to red and the tail flesh shrinks visibly from the shell. Lift them out of the pan onto a plate and continue to prepare the lobster according to the method on page 61.

3 Heat half the butter in the pan and fry the pieces of lobster head shell quickly until the color has changed, as before. Remove any of the flesh and set aside. Add the reserved shell from the tail with the onion, carrot and celery and cook for about 5 minutes, or until lightly browned. Add the wine and reduce by half before adding the brandy and the stock. Stir in the tomato paste and cook for 1 minute before adding the tomato halves. Cover the pan with a lid and, over gentle heat, cook for 20 minutes, or until the tomatoes are pulpy. While this is cooking, put the reserved coral and tomalley (liver) from the lobster into a blender with the remaining butter and blend until smooth.

4 Remove the lid from the pan, add the bouquet garni and the reserved fried claws and cook for 10 minutes. Lift out the claws and cool before cracking to remove the flesh.

5 Pass the tomato mixture through a strainer into a clean pan, discarding the shell, tomato skins, bouquet garni and diced vegetables. Cook the mixture, stirring occasionally, for 4 minutes, or until lightly syrupy.

6 Whisk the coral and tomalley flavored butter into the sauce until smooth, then add the lobster tail flesh and simmer very gently for 1 minute (if overcooked, the flesh with be tough). Remove the pan from the stove and leave the lobster tail to rest for 5 minutes in the sauce before removing and slicing into round slices. Gently rewarm the slices in the sauce with all the cracked claw and head meat. To serve, spoon onto hot plates and garnish with the parsley.

Chef's tips To make a bouquet garni, wrap the green part of a leek loosely around a bay leaf, a thyme sprig, some celery leaves and a few parsley stems, then tie with string, leaving a long tail for easy removal.

Lobsters generally have two large front claws. Although in some countries crayfish are also called spiny lobsters, they do not have the large front claws.

Sole meunière

A stylish classic: the sole is quickly pan-fried, then butter and lemon juice are poured over and the fish is eaten hot with parsley and lemon wedges. Dover sole is recommended for its firm texture and succulence, but any flat fish could be substituted.

*Total preparation time **10 minutes***
*Total cooking time **10 minutes***
Serves 4

**4 sole fillets, 1/4–1/2 lb. each,
  skin removed**
6 1/2 tablespoons clarified butter
2/3 cup seasoned flour
**6 1/2 teaspoons unsalted butter, chilled and
  cut into cubes**
1 tablespoon lemon juice, strained
**2 teaspoons finely chopped fresh parsley,
  to garnish**
1 lemon, cut into wedges, to garnish

1 Wash the fish, then dry well on paper towel. In a large frying pan, heat the clarified butter until hot.

2 Place the seasoned flour on a plate and roll the fillets in it to coat thoroughly, then pat off any excess. Place in the pan, skinned side up, and fry for about 2 minutes, turning once, or until lightly golden. Remove and place on hot plates.

3 Drain off the hot butter used for frying and wipe out the pan with paper towels before returning to the heat. Add the chilled butter to the pan and cook until golden and frothy. Remove from the stove, immediately add the lemon juice and, while still bubbling, spoon or pour over the fish.

4 Garnish with some parsley and serve immediately with the lemon wedges.

Basque-style tuna

Typically this Basque dish contains bell peppers, onions, tomatoes and ham—ideal ingredients to match the meaty texture of fresh tuna.

*Total preparation time **1 hour 5 minutes***
*Total cooking time **20 minutes***
Serves 4

2 or 3 ripe tomatoes, depending on size
3 tablespoons olive oil, or as needed
I tablespoon unsalted butter
4 pieces tuna fillet, 1/4–1/2 lb. each, skin removed
2 onions, thinly sliced
I small red bell pepper, thinly sliced
I small yellow bell pepper, thinly sliced
I small green bell pepper, thinly sliced
3 cloves garlic, finely chopped
1/2 cup dry white wine
I bouquet garni (see Chef's tip)
5 oz. Bayonne ham or prosciutto, thinly sliced and
    cut into 11/4-inch pieces
11/2 teaspoons chopped fresh parsley, to garnish

1 Bring a small saucepan of water to a boil. With the point of a sharp knife, score a small cross on the skin at the base of each tomato. Drop into the boiling water for 10 seconds, then plunge into a bowl of iced water. Peel the skin away from the cross, then cut around and remove the stem. Cut the tomatoes into quarters and

discard the seeds. Chop the flesh coarsely. You will need 11/4 cups. Set aside.

2 In a frying pan, heat 2 tablespoons of the oil and the butter. When foaming, add the tuna and fry over high heat for 1 minute on each side, or until lightly golden. Remove from the pan. Add the onions, cover and cook over low heat, stirring occasionally, for 3–4 minutes, or until soft but not colored. Add the bell peppers and garlic and cook gently for 1 minute, or until soft. Return the fish to the pan, add the tomatoes, wine, bouquet garni and some salt. Cover and simmer for 5 minutes.

3 Remove the tuna and cover with foil to keep warm. Bring the mixture in the pan to a boil and cook rapidly to reduce for 5 minutes, or until it lightly coats the back of a spoon. Season with pepper and a little more salt if necessary. Heat the remaining oil in a frying pan, add the ham, in batches, and quickly fry for 10 seconds on each side (you may need a little extra oil).

4 To serve, place the fish on plates and spoon the vegetable mixture over. Scatter the ham over or around the fish and sprinkle with the parsley.

Chef's tip To make a bouquet garni, wrap the green part of a leek loosely around a bay leaf, a thyme sprig, some celery leaves and a few parsley stems, then tie with string, leaving a long tail for easy removal.

Chef's techniques

◆

Shucking oysters

Use a shucker with a protection shield, and always protect the hand holding the oyster with a thick cloth.

Scrub the oysters in cold water. Place an oyster, rounded side down, on a thick, doubled cloth in the palm of your hand.

Insert an oyster knife through the pointed end of the oyster at the hinge where the top and bottom shells meet. Work the knife in until at least 1 1/4 inches is inside. Twist the knife to separate the shells.

Slide the knife between the oyster and the top shell, cut through the hinge muscle and remove the top shell.

Slide the knife between the oyster and the bottom shell to release it. Remove the oyster and tip any liquid through a cheesecloth-lined strainer into a bowl to get rid of any sand. Reserve the liquid.

Preparing shrimp

If using raw shrimp, remove the dark intestinal vein, which is unpleasant to eat.

Remove the shell, being careful to keep the flesh intact. Leave the tail end intact if specified in the recipe.

Make a shallow cut along the back of the shrimp with a small knife to expose the dark intestinal vein.

Remove the vein with the tip of the knife and discard. Rinse the shrimp and pat dry with a paper towel.

Preparing lobster bisque

The shell is an important part of the flavoring for this soup and is cooked with the meat.

Cut the lobsters in half lengthwise. Remove and discard the sac in the head and the vein down the center of the tail.

Twist off the claws and hit them with a rolling pin or the base of a small, heavy pan to crack them.

Using a large, sharp knife, cut across the tail into 3 or 4 pieces.

Killing a lobster

Place the lobster in the freezer for about 2 hours to desensitize it.

Hold the lobster, tail down, under a heavy cloth. Using a large, sharp knife, place the point in the center of the head and quickly pierce through to the cutting board, cutting down and forward between the eyes.

Preparing lobster Américaine

Depending on the type of lobster you have, the claws will vary in size.

Twist and remove the two main claws, if applicable, from where they meet the body. Separate the head from the tail. Cook the claws and tail according to the method in the recipe.

Remove the flesh from the tail by snipping with scissors around the edge of the flat undershell and lifting it away.

Using your fingers, gently ease the flesh out of the tail in one piece. Reserve the shell.

With a large, sharp knife, split the head in two lengthwise. Remove and reserve any coral (roe) and green-gray tomalley (liver). Discard the stomach sac found behind the mouth. Chop the head shell into large pieces.

Cleaning mussels

Mussels must be very carefully cleaned and should be stored in the refrigerator under a damp cloth.

Clean the mussels by scrubbing the shells with a brush to remove any sand. Scrape any barnacles off with a knife.

Pull off any beards from the mussels.

Discard any mussels that are broken, are not tightly closed or do not close when lightly tapped on a work surface.

Filleting flatfish

Filleting your own fish is simple when you know how—just use a good sharp knife.

Lay the fish dark side up. Cut around the outside of the fish with a filleting knife where the flesh meets the fins.

Cut down the center of the fish from head to tail with a sharp knife. Make sure you cut all the way through to the bone.

Working from the center of the fillet to the edge, cut away one fillet with long, broad strokes of the knife, without leaving too much flesh. Remove the other fillet in the same way, then turn the fish over and repeat.

Cleaning scallops

If the scallops are in their shells, remove them by sliding a knife under the white muscle and orange roe.

Wash the scallops to remove any grit or sand, then pull away the small, tough, shiny white muscle and the black vein. If the orange roe is attached, leave intact.

Skinning fish

Get the angle of the knife against the skin right and removing the skin will then be easy.

Lay the fillet skin side down and cut across the flesh at the tail. Dip your fingers in salt to get a good grip, grasp the tail and, starting at the cut, work the knife away from you at a shallow angle using a sawing action.

Filleting round fish

Choose the freshest fish and fillet them yourself to be sure of the best-quality cut.

Using a filleting knife, cut off the fins and cut out the gills behind the head and discard.

Make a small cut at the bottom of the stomach, then cut along the underside, stopping just below the gills. Pull the innards out and discard. Wash the fish.

Make a cut around the back of the head, then working from head to tail, cut along the backbone. Holding the knife flat, use long strokes to cut away the flesh, then pull the flesh away from the bones.

Pin boning fish

Salmon or other fish, such as sea bass, often have small bones left in them. These need to be removed.

Run the fingers of your hand along the flesh, pressing lightly to find the bones. Using a pair of tweezers or your fingers, remove any fine pin bones.

Serving a salmon

Place the cooked salmon on a piece of waxed paper before you begin.

Using a sharp knife, cut the skin just above the tail, then cut through the skin along the back and in front of the gills. Using the knife to help you, work from head to tail to peel off and discard the skin.

Place a serving plate under one side of the waxed paper and flip the fish over onto the plate, using the paper to help you. Remove the rest of the skin. Remove the head if preferred.

Scrape away any dark flesh with a knife. Split down the center of the top fillet, then carefully remove and lay the two quarter fillets on each side of the salmon.

Lift out the backbone by peeling it back from the head end. Snip it with scissors just before the tail. Remove any other stray bones and lift up and replace the two fillets.

First published in the United States in 2000 by Periplus Editions (HK) Ltd., with editorial offices at
153 Milk Street, Boston, Massachusetts 02109.

Murdoch Books and Le Cordon Bleu thank the 32 masterchefs of all the Le Cordon Bleu Schools, whose knowledge and
expertise have made this book possible, especially: Chef Terrien, Chef Boucheret, Chef Duchêne (MOF), Chef Guillut,
Chef Pinaud, Paris; Chef Males, Chef Walsh, Chef Power, Chef Neveu, Chef Paton, Chef Poole-Gleed, Chef Wavrin, London;
Chef Chantefort, Chef Nicaud, Chef Jambert, Chef Honda, Tokyo; Chef Salambien, Chef Boutin, Chef Harris, Sydney;
Chef Lawes, Adelaide; Chef Guiet, Chef Denis, Chef Petibon, Chef Jean Michel Poncet, Ottawa.
Of the many students who helped the Chefs test each recipe, a special mention to graduates Hollace Hamilton and Alice Buckley.
A very special acknowledgment to Helen Barnard, Alison Oakervee and Deepika Sukhwani, who have been responsible for the
coordination of the Le Cordon Bleu team throughout this series under the Presidency of André Cointreau.

First published in Australia in 1999 by Murdoch Books®

Series Manager: Kay Halsey
Series Concept, Design and Art Direction: Juliet Cohen
Food Editor: Lulu Grimes
Designer: Michelle Cutler
Photographer: Joe Filshie
Food Stylist: Carolyn Fienberg
Food Preparation: Justine Poole
Chef's Techniques Photographer: Reg Morrison
Home Economists: Anna Beaumont, Michaela Le Compte, Tracey Meharg, Justine Poole

Library of Congress catalog card number: 99-068927
ISBN 962-593-823-0

Front cover: Garlic shrimp

Distributed in the United States by
Tuttle Publishing
Distribution Center
Airport Industrial Park
364 Innovation Drive
North Clarendon, VT 05759-9436
Tel: (802) 773-8930
Tel: (800) 526-2778

PRINTED IN SINGAPORE

06 05 04 03 02 01 00 10 9 8 7 6 5 4 3 2 1

Important: Some of the recipes in this book may include raw eggs, which can cause salmonella poisoning.
Those who might be at risk from this (the elderly, pregnant women, young children and those suffering
from immune deficiency diseases) should check with their physicians before eating raw eggs.